Everything I Know
I Learned from
Home Improvement

Artwork by
Susie Muise

Text by
Hope Lyda

HARVEST HOUSE PUBLISHER
EUGENE, OREGON

D1457959

Everything I Know I Learned from Home Improvement

Text Copyright © 2005 by Harvest House Publishers
Eugene, Oregon 97402

ISBN 0-7369-1489-7

All works of art appearing in this book are copyrighted by Susie Muise and licensed by Courtney Davis, Inc., San Francisco, California, and may not be reproduced without permission.

Design and Production by Garborg Design Works, Minneapolis, Minnesota

Unless otherwise indicated, all Scripture quotations are taken from the HOLY BIBLE, NEW INTERNATIONAL VERSION®. NIV®. Copyright©1973, 1978, 1984 by the International Bible Society. Used by permission of Zondervan. All rights reserved.

All rights reserved. No part of this publication may be reproduced, stored in a retrieval system, or transmitted in any form or by any means—electronic, mechanical, digital, photocopy, recording, or any other—except for brief quotations in printed reviews, without the prior permission of the publisher.

Printed in China

05 06 07 08 09 10 11 12 / IM / 8 7 6 5 4 3 2 1

What is this thrall for houses? I come from a long line of women who open their handbags and take out swatches of upholstery material, colored squares of bathroom tile, seven shades of yellow paint samples, and strips of flowered wallpaper. We love the concept of four walls. "What is her house like?" my sister asks, and we both know she means what is she like.

FRANCES MAYES
Under the Tuscan Sun

3

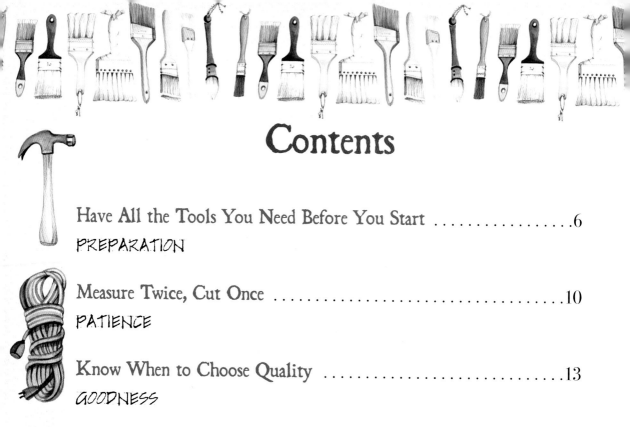

Contents

Have All the Tools You Need Before You Start 6
PREPARATION

Measure Twice, Cut Once 10
PATIENCE

Know When to Choose Quality 13
GOODNESS

Putting Up Walls Can Bring Them Down 16
PEACE

Mistakes Create Possibilities 23
SELF-CONTROL

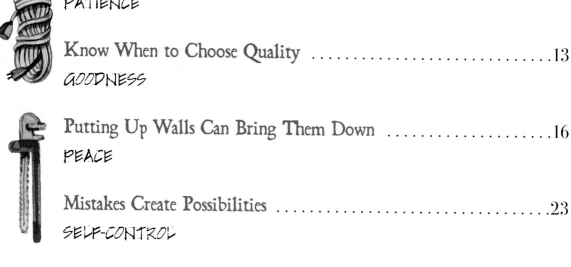

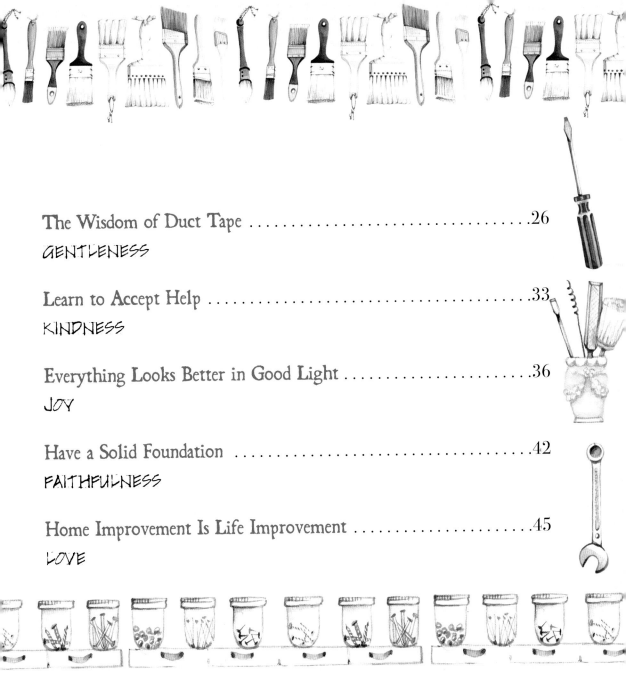

The Wisdom of Duct Tape 26
GENTLENESS

Learn to Accept Help 33
KINDNESS

Everything Looks Better in Good Light .36
JOY

Have a Solid Foundation 42
FAITHFULNESS

Home Improvement Is Life Improvement 45
LOVE

Have All the Tools You Need Before You Start

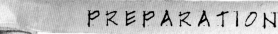

PREPARATION

Instead of a potted fern or a personalized welcome mat, I think the mandatory house warming or "congratulations, you are an adult" gift should be a toolbox filled with the basics. I know I could have used that. Maybe it is just too clunky to fit in a cellophane gift bag. Or people think it would be offensive to suggest that neither I nor my husband had a dowry including hardware. But a toolbox is a way to welcome a person into (or warn them of) a life of minor projects, planned adventures, and unexpected repairs.

New parents lament the fact that children do not come with instruction manuals. I say "woe to all adults" because grown-up existence does not come with a life toolbox.

Wouldn't it be nice if we knew just which handy item to use to twist, turn, or straight-en every situation we face? These complex gadgets would be well-labeled so we would not affix the very thing meant to be removed, nor toss the situation meant to be restored.

The professional contractor and the weekend home improvement putterer can offer the same

sage advice when it comes to tools...have what you need before you start a project.

If you ever wasted enthusiasm intended for a day of projects on making calls to borrow a saw, a non-shedding paint brush, a thing-a-ma-jig you saw on television, then you know the cost of not being prepared—by the time you get the tools lined up, your window of productivity has been sealed shut by drying paint.

Life projects can feel the same way. We watch chances for growth or happiness pass us by because we aren't quite prepared. We meant to work on our patience. We intended to set some goals. We almost prayed for direction but became distracted by the weather report, a trip to the dentist, and the price of gasoline. And the next trial or opportunity appears, and there aren't

enough coping tools in the shed, so to speak.

We seem slow to learn the secret that home improvement projects share with us...make the mistake once (okay, maybe twice), and then get prepared. Bottom line: Store up knowledge, wisdom, and experience so you can succeed.

Determining and Gathering the Tools

The good news is it can be great fun to gather the tools you need to take care of yourself and your home. In my life, I liken it to the childhood wonder of acquiring school supplies. My journey up and down the aisles of the local drugstore was filled with life's delights. A crisp, three-subject notebook meant potential in new areas. A set of pencils not yet marred by bite marks inspired repentance. And we all know

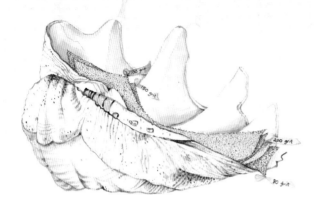

Hammer: a source of strength
Measuring Tape: a way to see how far you have come and to set your milestones
Nails: certainty—a way to secure a situation
Sandpaper: patience and the grit of perseverance to smooth out the rough edges
Saw: discernment to cut through the hard stuff
Level: a way to find balance

the phenomena of a fresh box of crayons—infinite possibilities.

An equally inspired trip to the local home improvement center or hardware store offers the same thrill. Or, to stay true to a homeowner's budget, you can acquire tools from different sources over time. Keep a running list of what you need, so you can quickly gather the basics from garage or estate sales, seasonal discount sales at stores, and the occasional donation by a friend or family member who has upgraded their cache.

As I gathered what I wanted to have in my toolbox, I noticed how each item served a purpose which mirrored a need in my life. Filling the fire-engine red metal chest, I made a mental checklist of the tools essential to shape a good life.

And so on. Here was a definite life lesson in the making. These physical tools, and many others, remind us of the spiritual tools that are to be collected, taken care of, and manifested in our lives. In the Bible they are called the fruit of the spirit: "love, joy, peace, patience, kindness, goodness, faithfulness, gentleness and self-control" (Galatians 5:22-23). And they do indeed take a lifetime to gather.

As we explore the physical act of home improvement projects, let's also consider how these characteristics take shape. We will be ready the next time we have to fix a leak or mend a broken heart.

In My Dad's Toolbox

(A.K.A. DUKE'S DOZEN TOOLS)

1. level
2. hammer
3. wire cutters
4. screwdriver
5. square
6. safety goggles
7. small saw
8. tape measure
9. drill
10. pliers
11. crescent wrench
12. pry bar

And tucked behind your ear:
always a carpenter's pencil.

Every toolbox should include an emergency flare as well
as the phone numbers of a reliable handyman and the local hospital.

TERRY GLASPEY
The Un-Do-It-Yourselfer, who has a bad fence to prove it

Measure Twice, Cut Once

PATIENCE

As children, we are told to be patient—ask your other parent, say you are sorry again and *mean it*, wait until after dinner to eat that cake, etc.—so when we become card-carrying members of the adult world, we like to cut corners on occasion.

But I beg of you, do not practice the act of impatience when you are doing home improvements. Before you draw the teeth of a saw across a perfectly fine piece of wood please follow this patience-in-projects rule: Measure twice, cut once.

Why is this rule so important? For one thing, transporting wood causes it to shrink. It is one of those home improvement urban myths that seems to hold. For example, my brother-in-law Don is a very fix-it kind of guy. He likes doing a task once and well.

He measured a piece of molding at the store and was thrilled that it would cover trim for two windows. When he returned home he unloaded the wood, checked the mail, said hi to his son, Ben, went to his chop saw, and...cut. That second round of measuring...*not* on the list of things he did.

His perfectly centered cut left him with not one but two pieces of molding that were...you guessed it...too short to be placed over those barren windows. Urban myth perpetuated and another trip to the store required.

It is important to know that the measure twice, cut once rule only works if you know *what* you are measuring. Case in point...a friend's uncle had a splendid boat that was in need of shelter. He carefully measured that splendid boat and set out to build a boat house using those precise measurements. Using the *actual* measurements of what you want a structure to hold is not going to work. (Hopefully, that does not require much explanation.) Sadly, as they transported the boat, it did not shrink. Today, the boat looks grand covered with a tarp and setting just outside that structure (now referred to as a tool shed).

Patience does not come easily for most of us. We cannot eyeball how much patience it might take to raise a kid, coach pee-wee soccer, write a book, love our spouse. Whatever the amount of patience we

> ## A man's wisdom gives him patience.
> THE BOOK OF PROVERBS

think we need...we probably need double. The discipline that it takes to measure just one more time is the same as the discipline and diligence it takes to tell yourself (just one more time) that a situation requires extra patience.

Measuring twice means you are less likely to say, "I have to go to the store and buy this piece of trim...again." And practicing patience...measuring your response twice (or more)...means you are less likely to say, "I am sorry." Maybe those childhood lessons were not "suburban myths" adults used to control us but were real life lessons to make us better, kinder adults.

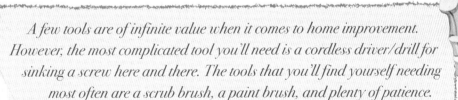

A few tools are of infinite value when it comes to home improvement. However, the most complicated tool you'll need is a cordless driver/drill for sinking a screw here and there. The tools that you'll find yourself needing most often are a scrub brush, a paint brush, and plenty of patience.

INTRODUCTION FROM *Home Improvement All-In-One for Dummies*

After assembling various pieces of furniture from various different makers, I learned to stick with one that consistently provides quality pieces, quality instructions, and quality customer service. Likewise with my tools. Once I find a manufacturer that makes good tools, I stick with them. Price no longer becomes an issue. My time and emotions are worth more than a few cents or dollars saved by buying from an inferior supplier.

BEV HARRISON
Queen of Quality

Know When to Choose Quality

GOODNESS

Trial and error. Ouch. Any of us who have ventured into home improvement waters know that trial and error can become costly. The trick is knowing when to wing it—go for the inexpensive material or solution—and when to go all out. Among other things, it depends on your personal priorities for this project...money, time, quality?

If you decide to hire out, and you are fortunate to find the right person, you will be privileged to watch a true craftsman. That can be a wonderful gift to yourself.

I needed a transitional piece of wood to smooth out the line between two rooms with different flooring. I just kept throwing rugs over it and ignoring it. Then when I was on a home improvement hiring roll, I added that project to the list.

No Regrets

The difference between me and the professional I hired is that I did not have a clue what to envision for that transition. And he, with years of experience and skill-honing, envisioned this wonderful piece of maple with a gentle curve that blended the slightly different heights in the rooms. It was smooth, sleek, and beautiful. I would have created makeshift and the craftsman

> When you hire a professional consider that part of the fee goes to your education. Try to notice how this expert does things—the tools and steps involved in a project. What special power tools might you rent to do this job?
>
> DAVID J. TENENBAUM
> *Complete Idiot's Guide to Home Repair and Maintenance*

created magic. I loved the outcome so much I had dreams of throwing wads of cash at him so he could stay and repair all the little things that drive me crazy about my house.

When we choose materials, tools, and professional assistance that is high caliber, we are choosing goodness. Rarely do people regret going for quality.

The trial-and -error choices you make in your home present the same quandaries that life presents. But when we strive for goodness, we will face sacrifices but rarely regrets. This formula will only improve the value of the life you are shaping.

Home improvement projects have taught me the importance of counting the cost. And still I rarely get it right—projects always seem to take more time and money than I expect them to. But I plan ahead, jump in with both feet, and hope for the best.

Maybe it's best this way. I might not start a project if I really knew what it was going to cost me. Maybe I'm better off processing projects—and life—a little bit at a time.

GENE SKINNER
Putterer

Putting Up Walls
Can Bring them Down

PEACE

Though I have never looked into Feng Shui, I certainly believe that the arrangement of objects and space can inspire the sense of peace in the home. I choose to open or fill areas to change the flow of my main rooms and to suit my mood. Sometimes I want quiet, secure places that have protective, defined perimeters. When in social moods, I want the room wide open to welcome others to the home sanctuary.

Hardwood floors are a space-arrangers dream. You can move the end table right of center, shove the buffet to the left, and nudge the bookshelf to the corner...all without breaking a sweat. Recently I had just the excuse to rearrange...my in-laws were coming to visit from Texas for a week. Gleefully I glided room to room with pieces of furniture like a pairs-skating finalist.

I successfully carved out cozy nooks so we could all enjoy personal times of reading, resting, and conversation. My work was done. I spent the last day watching my husband run errands and use up nervous energy. His anticipation of stepping back into the role of child and eldest son involved mental rearranging.

My mother- and father-in-law arrived, and we all settled into the house easily, making our way into temporary routines to fill the space of time. I intended to have plenty of catch-up chats with my mother-in-law as we went on walks or sat across from one another at local coffee shops. But Marc and his dad both require much more busyness. In Lyda family language, the words "itinerary" and "vacation" are actually used in the same sentence.

So I was not surprised when father and son measured the entryway several

---

Moving Furniture Alone

You shouldn't do it...but if you do...on slick floors slide the furniture onto a rubber-backed bath mat that you've turned over. The furniture will stick to the rubber, and the fabric side will glide along the floor. On carpet put a couple of aluminum or tin pie plates under the legs of the piece for reduced drag as you push.

BETTY "FIX-IT" FLETCHER

times and headed to the home improvement store. They returned with ample supplies for a yet unannounced endeavor. Just recently, Marc and I had discussed several areas of our home in need of attention, so I imagined crossing something off that to-do list...making space for new ideas.

But as the men dismantled my cozy nooks to make room for 2 x 4s, levels, and nail guns, the project was disclosed...and it was not on that to-do list. They were building a wall to divide the entry from the dining area.

A wall? What about the...? And the...? Or the rewiring of the...? My mind toured the many repairs and renovations our old house really needed. And a wall was not among them. I stammered to state my case for the other ideas, but I could see the fellows were already in a zone. As the two prepared to put up the framing, I broke through my wall of silence with occasional passive-aggressive sighs.

What Goes Up, Must Come Down

Marc and his dad worked side by side, often in silence. There were times of agreement, disagreement, and decision-making. Work was their form of communication. I think a lot of nodding and shrugging took place. Slowly they found their way around and alongside each other, bridging the gaps created by time, distance, and change.

Gradually, as the great wall went up my measly defenses came down. The crew of two added special touches as they formed the new structure. An arched cutout in the center

> The Lord gives strength to his people; the Lord blesses his people with peace.
>
> THE BOOK OF PSALMS

matched the one in our living room for a peaceful symmetry. Bookshelves lined the lower half of the wall, and two marbled, amber-hued lights illuminated the newly created corner for reading or dining.

At the end of each day we stepped over the sprawl of tools, swept up the dust, and noted the emerging creation where there once was nothing. The new wall was not dividing up our room, as I had feared, but was gathering random areas into whole and functional spaces.

Pictures of that project-in-process technically show what it takes to put up walls. Memories of that project reveal what it takes to bring them down...a labor of love that gathers the separated space between parent and child, father and son, and makes it whole.

Jobs for Meager-Beavers

(THE BEGINNERS)

Drywall and plaster—repairing small holes
Unclogging drains, fixing running toilets
    and leaky valves
Painting, staining, applying polyurethane
    and varnish
Prepping—sanding and caulking
Replacing windowpanes
Installing subflooring

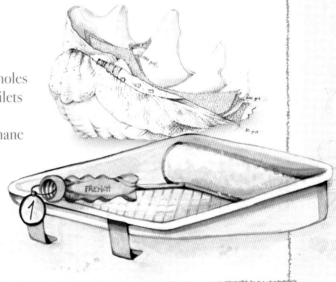

TY PENNINGTON,
carpenter on TLC's *Trading Spaces*
Ty's Tricks

My wife, Cindy, has always appreciated my abilities to fix and construct things, but the problem was one of priority. Most of my projects have involved something that Cindy wants to have done, but often I have not done them in the order or way she would like. To put it frankly, I have resisted her wishes. This has led to major conflict—such as the time I pruned the apple trees instead of working on the bathroom plumbing.

I always felt the struggle over household work was as much her problem as mine. Finally, after one big blow-up, I admitted it was mostly my problem. I told her she could set the project priorities, and I would listen to her wishes on how things were to be done.

If this seems like a simple principle, it is. If it seems simple to put into action, it's not. And maybe it applies only in one direction: a husband doing things for his wife. But it's really lessened the "discussions" we have over home improvements.

And now—though it might seem surprising to the relationally uninitiated—I enjoy my "hobby" a lot more.

PAUL GOSSARD
Husband First, Home Handyman Second

The Bee
antiques ...

©Susie Muive

Mistakes Create Possibilities

SELF-CONTROL

"And why did you remove the counter?" I asked with poorly masked frustration. My husband and I were looking at the rather large chunk of exposed sub-flooring in between our kitchen and our dining area. We both were puzzled. He, because the crater looked more daunting than he had envisioned when first taking a crowbar to the former counter. I, because when I had left an hour earlier, my husband had been passively eating breakfast.

We stared at each other over the chasm.

"We have more room in the kitchen now," he offered.

I acknowledged the truth in this statement. We now had room for...a fire pit. A hot tub. A wine cellar. I like more

room...but I knew it would be a long time before this hole was ever fixed, filled, or made functional. And to reinforce my conclusion, Demolition Man took off his cape, wiped his brow, and decided to make a sandwich.

We temporarily covered the gap with a piece of plywood which didn't lie flat. So we slid the refrigerator on top to weigh it down. We were able to ignore it completely until one day I noticed how much dirt and bread crumb debris was accumulating in the crevices around the plank. Away came the levels of camouflage, and this time Marc was ready to stare down his troubled creation. He measured. He nudged. He pulled. And he made a remarkable discovery.

The abyss, it seemed, was not a pit of darkness. It was the opening to a tunnel of light. That horrific expanse of linoleum floor that stretched from our front door through our dining area and up to our kitchen sink had been covering a secret. Looking closely at the fault line, we saw edges of the same beautiful hardwood flooring that blessed the rest of our home.

> It is all very well to plan our ideal house or apartment, our individual castle in Spain, but it isn't necessary to have any intolerable furnishings just because we cannot realize our castle. There never was a house so bad it couldn't be made over into something worthwhile.
>
> ELSIE DE WOLF
> *The House in Good Taste*

stretched two feet, we were about to turn our would-be fire pit into a sunken living room. And if the wood we exposed had been covered for a darn good reason we would need to shop for a very big rug.

It was therapeutic to tear into the pressboard. Apparently the former owners had not believed gravity would do its job, because the board was glued and nailed to the floor. But we had a chance to turn this around for good. We were thrilled to find that the wood extended all the way to the front door.

This seemed too good to be true. Could one moment of passionate destruction turn into a chance for a brilliant floor makeover? We believed yes.

So we took a risk. This time it was more calculated than my husband's first effort of "pull up and ask questions later." But nevertheless, with crowbars, hammers, and glue solvent we attacked the icky floor not knowing what we would find. If that bit of wood only

Learning Our Lessons

Impulse anything, from shopping to arguing, can lead to grave mistakes...the kind you find difficult to dig yourself out of. Such lack of self-control inspires urges to

24

expend energy without having any plan for the outcome. But instead of covering up the mistake, take a little time to learn the lesson. Then return to the scene of the crime and figure out how to redeem it. The half-removed deck you could not stand another minute or the painted wall you thought would capture the sunny disposition of a daffodil are no longer mistakes but chances for transformation.

Those fascinating home décor shows on television and cable make it difficult to sit back and do nothing when there are a billion-and-one things we could tear apart, redecorate, or update. We all want a makeover because it feels like starting over. Yet we forget that real change requires planning and hard work.

I will state the obvious: *Practicing self-control rather than taking a hammer to the counter on a whim is the mature thing.* But it is not often our nature. Still, we can sharpen the tool of self-control when we go back and fix whatever part of our home or life we have offended. We can heal it, make it better than ever, and respect the full process of transformation—including the hard work.

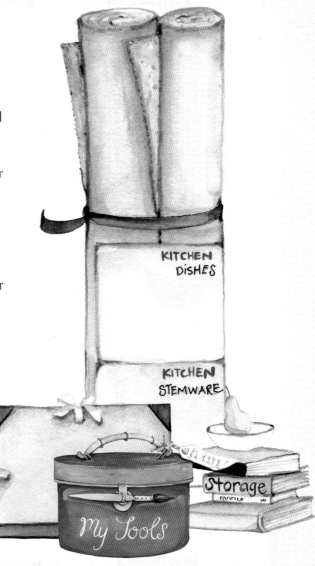

KITCHEN DISHES

KITCHEN STEMWARE

My Tools

Storage

The Wisdom of Duct Tape

GENTLENESS

While home improvement efforts often involve hard work, there are times when they should be easy...simple even... and can be approached in a gentle way. "The shortest distance between two points is a straight line" is not only an answer on the geometry quiz...it is a truth that can be applied to your home and life journeys as well.

If we get worked up about a task and spend countless hours fretting or preparing, we might simply be missing the gentle solution. Power tools turn some people into power junkies. Power in all forms—brute force, loads of money, tools, etc.—does not always simplify the job. And it can pull the plug on our creativity.

Approach your next task with this thought in mind: There is a simple way to do this. Perhaps it is not always true...but it is freeing to let yourself start with simplicity. This is the duct-tape philosophy from college days. You know...your pants need to be hemmed. The only thread-like item you own is dental floss. You have ten minutes to get to Western Civilization. So, you use duct tape. Duct tape solutions may not be the

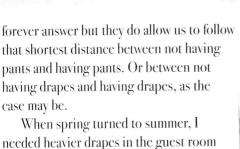

forever answer but they do allow us to follow that shortest distance between not having pants and having pants. Or between not having drapes and having drapes, as the case may be.

When spring turned to summer, I needed heavier drapes in the guest room to prevent the sun from turning the place into a sauna. So using my duct tape mindset, I went to my favorite store...my own home...and shoplifted the sturdy drapes from the living room. Now to provide window covering for my living room I went to a local discount store and found an oversized linen table cloth. Carefully I cut a slit in each end of the double edged hem so I could slide the drapery pole through the entire length (which would become the width). And I didn't do anything to this cloth that would

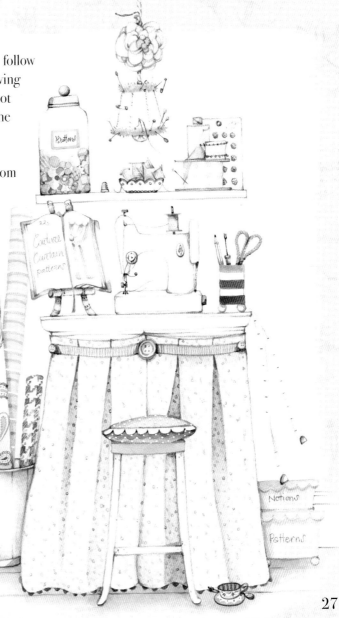

27

undermine its original purpose.

Once creativity is opened up it is hard to hold back. This happens every time you let yourself be a duct tape diva.

Simplicity in Action

Recently I had to relocate my home office...from one end of the house to the other. I had kept things in disarray for quite some time. The random file folders, piles of books, and tangles of electrical cords strangled the energy out of me each time I entered the new office.

But with my mind opened to the way of

> Determine what sort of a house will be fit for you; determine to work for it, to get it...one that you can entirely enjoy and manage, but which you will not be proud of except as you make it charming in its modesty.
>
> JOHN RUSKIN

gentle solutions, I poured myself a cup of coffee, and faced the room. What is the simple way? Ding. A simple solution comes to mind. I stole the rug from the living room to get me started. Once in the office, the rug anchored the room so it felt solid instead of scattered. Much better. From there it was easy. I moved the desk in front of the window. I swiped two pieces of art from the spare room in the house. A floor lamp that was pretty much decorative in one room became quite functional in this space. I put files in the file drawer and shoved extra stuff into the closet

28

to deal with later. (Simplicity does not mean you will be cured of procrastination.)

Now this is a room I want to enter each morning. As I sit before my computer, I watch the trees sway in the springtime breeze. My bare feet rest on the color block rug (a terrible design in a shirt but great for a floor covering). Not bad for a morning's efforts.

We either are or know people who do things the hard way. Everything is a chore. Every decision requires at least seven rounds of pro/con lists. Change is difficult. But once we learn how to be gentle with ourselves and our tasks, life does become more pleasurable.

As I was enjoying the look of my new living room "curtains," it occurred to me that I was sitting on the comfy rocking chair that I reupholstered using tacks and...you guessed it...duct tape. Ahhh, the full circle of simplicity.

The Duct Tape Diva Dozen

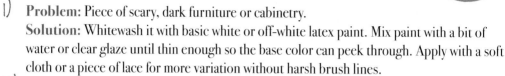

1) **Problem:** Piece of scary, dark furniture or cabinetry.
   Solution: Whitewash it with basic white or off-white latex paint. Mix paint with a bit of water or clear glaze until thin enough so the base color can peek through. Apply with a soft cloth or a piece of lace for more variation without harsh brush lines.

2) **Problem:** Need curtains to reflect change of season, color scheme, or holiday theme.
   Solution: Purchase two packs of clip-on curtain rings. Buy or use one to two tablecloths of your liking, clip on the rings, and slide onto the curtain rod. Short windows: use length of tablecloth as width. Large windows: use two to three 84″ rectangular cloths hung vertically.

3) **Problem:** Your picture frames are taking over your coffee table.
   Solution: Have a piece of table-top glass cut to fit your coffee table (a service available at many glass/window stores), arrange loose photos flat on table, then place glass on top.

4) **Problem:** Your bathroom has no personality.
   Solution: Get rid of that large, industrial mirror above the sink and replace with a style usually found elsewhere in the home—antiques, white washed, oval, or one of those rectangular mirrors with small hooks that are usually used as an entry way coat rack (these hooks are great for hand towels).

5) **Problem:** You are bored with your home.
   Solution: Go to the paint store and choose a color that makes your day. Head home and paint a room or a wall in this great new color. If you have painter's regret a month from now...change it. That is the brilliance of paint!

6) **Problem:** You don't know diddly.
   Solution: Grab a coffee and head to one of those do-it-yourself sessions hosted by a local home improvement store. Even if you don't need a new patio or *need* to install a fence, the details about working with materials and tools start to sink in.

7) **Problem:** You want a new living room look but cannot afford a major overhaul.
Solution: Determine a complementary color to freshen your room, then purchase three new throw pillows, a table runner to drape over a table or chair, and then either paint one piece of furniture or purchase a rug that emphasizes the new color.

8) **Problem:** Your tool stash is dismal.
Solution: Next birthday or gift-giving season throw yourself a do-it-yourself shower. Even register at stores for tools you want to have on hand. People love knowing what to get you and it is divine to stock up on things you really need.

9) **Problem:** You have a horrific baby blue bathtub.
Solution: Get over it. Decide you *love* baby blue and find a rug and towel color scheme that pairs baby blue with a color you *really* love.

10) **Problem:** Your walls are bare.
Solution: Fill space with: rescued old window frames painted, enlarged photos in inexpensive frames, plants that reach into the visual space of the wall, tiered shelving that can hold frames, table runners attached to a dowel at the top and draped vertically (arrange in a series of three for a rather royal feel).

11) **Problem:** Your kitchen is very outdated.
Solution: Change up curtains, rugs, towels, and canisters. Add a piece of framed art and a stylish bar stool/chair that serves kitchen visitors or as a surface space. Place a stylish cutting board on your counter for a splash of color. Budget permitting, change the cupboard/drawer pulls for an amazingly simple makeover.

12) **Problem:** You are hosting Thanksgiving and have a table for two.
Solution: Long piece of pressboard placed over simple saw horses (if you have casual company or a long tablecloth to cover them) or if the length can be centered over your small table, do that and brace it in place with tucked away C-clamps or, of course...duct tape.

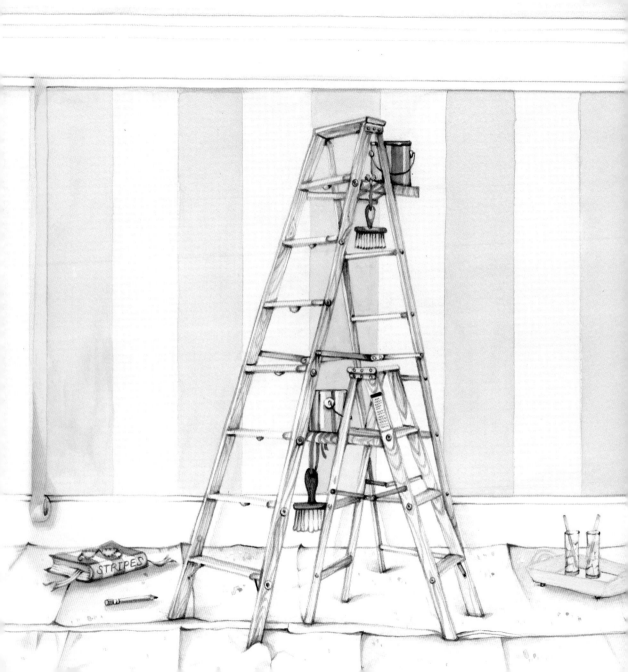

Learn to Accept Help

KINDNESS

I was fortunate to receive the graciousness of others before I even moved into my home. Thankfully two friends and co-workers, Betty and Barb, understood a basic principle for life and for home ownership...there are times when you need help. Sometimes you know enough to ask for it and sometimes others care enough to offer.

Our basic ranch style home thankfully has redeeming characteristics: coved ceilings, arched entryways, great hardwood floors. When we bought our home, those floors were stained the color of tobacco and were in desperate need of refinishing. Focused on just getting out of our apartment and into the spaciousness of a home, we figured we would just do it later (which would have been a nightmare). Enter smart, kind friends. They came over to see our place and eagerly shared in our love for the house. At the end of the quick tour they looked at each other, then to us, and offered to refinish our floors as a housewarming gift. I couldn't believe it. My husband was silent, and I was ready to protest... it was too big. How could we ever repay them? Their answer, "pass on help to another

when the chance arises."
We accepted their extreme
generosity and within days
our floor was sanded and
refinished with the most
amazing TLC.

It can be humbling to
receive such a gift of help,
but the act of receiving help
opens you up to God's
blessings in your life.

A Dream Brought to Life

Two years ago I drew a
diagram of a pergola on a
Starbucks napkin. I saw it in
the left corner of our large
back yard. I envisioned how
we would build and enjoy
such an outdoor space.
Months went by. We talked
of making the effort but we
did not make headway until
Marc's mom, Julia, rented
us a small Bobcat to dig out
the back corner.

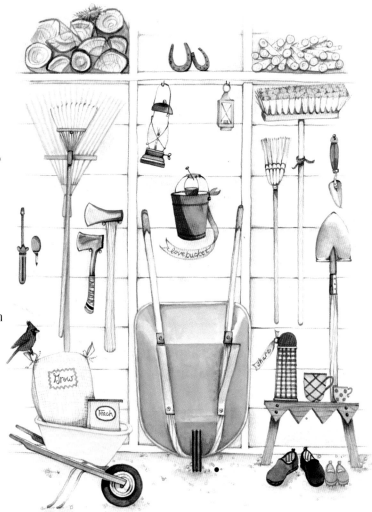

For several more months we watched six-foot-tall weeds fill that de-grassed piece of our back forty. Then one Saturday my husband took the napkin and a measuring tape and began the hard work of digging the post holes.

The dream returned and kindnesses came to us one by one to see it through. My father helped us set the posts and pour concrete. My sister, brother-in-law, and nephew came down for a weekend visit bearing the gifts of a table saw, free labor, and great patience. Two years later, that napkin etching became a three dimensional monument honoring the generosity of others.

When people comment on our beautiful floors, it is a joy to recount the story of two friends who gave of their time, sweat, and resources to make those floors possible. When my friends and family gather in the open air structure, now scented and shaded with climbing roses, evergreen clematis, and jasmine, I think of every hand and heart that brought it into being. And I cannot wait to pass gifts of such kindness on to others.

My dad always believed that I could do anything that my brothers could do, so he never treated me like a girl when it came to do-it-yourself projects. He and I built a loft bed for my daughters, and it is one of my most treasured memories. Also, my father-in-law realized early in my marriage to his son that I was the mechanical one. One Christmas he gave us a saber saw and told me that one of these days he was going to give me a creeper so that I could get under the car without getting on the ground. He never did, but his comment validated me, and I always appreciated it. And, my husband is never embarrassed or intimidated by my mechanical skill where his is lacking. He is a liberated man! All the men in my life are an encouragement, rather than a detriment, to me.

BEV HARRISON
Happy Do-It-Yourselfer

35

Everything Looks Better in Good Light

JOY

Casting a life situation in good light helps us view our circumstances with optimism and with a chance for joy. We might have an argument about who left dirt on the carpet, but a brighter attitude helps us realize the mess can be cleaned up and no harm was done. Later when we find out the dog did it, and not our spouse, we can be thankful that we kept the discussion light. Now the only one in the doghouse is the dog.

We can offer our family and guests an inner joy if we bathe them in the radiance and warmth of proper lighting. How many of us probably experience a bit of the blues because we do not let enough good light into our homes and our lives at all times?

Those of us who have called a cubicle or corporate office "home" know how sharp overhead light can make you feel like a slice of pepperoni pizza waiting to be chosen in the deli case. The other end of the spectrum is the murky lighting that makes everyone appear seasick. Think of Tom Hank's character in the movie *Joe Versus the Volcano* where he sits in the dank office bathed in light as illuminating as sludge. His mental state is clearly *not* joyful.

Low lighting or a bright glare immediately cause our features to frown as we strive to see...from there it is easy to slip into the mood that fits the face. So joy and good lighting can be found somewhere in between

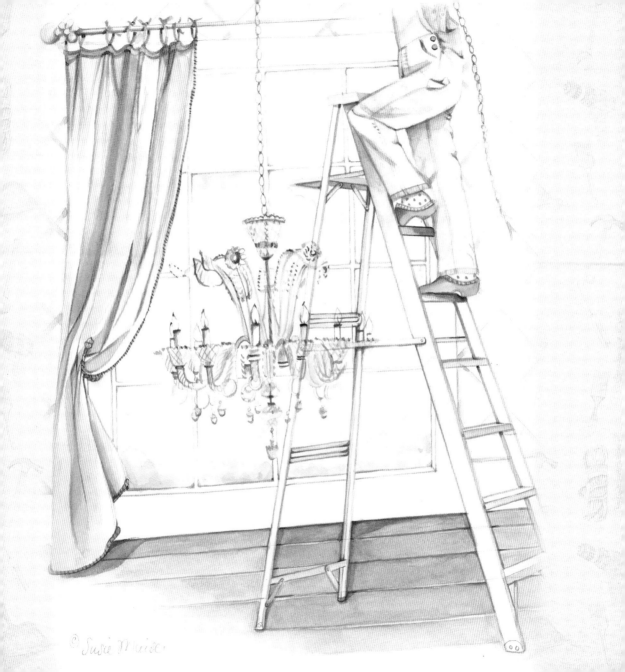

© Susie Maine

these two extreme levels.

What is good lighting? A simple way to assess the joy level of your home is to consider the F.A.B. lighting factors: Functional, Aesthetic, and Blended.

Functional

The function of a space will determine the function of the lighting. The corner of a room might be a reading nook while the central area accommodates the activity of

gatherings. Your overhead light might help you see the way to the couch or chair, but it alone cannot serve the function of most rooms.

Figure out what you need and where you need it. A floor lamp with adjustable height could service the reading chair. A simple, one-bulb soft light on the entry table can help you find your keys in the early morning without waking the whole house. If a room holds a prized work of art, cabinet of collectibles, or a beautifully carved mantel piece, a more intense, directed light could serve as a gentle spotlight.

Each element of light should serve a function in the overall feel and purpose of a room's space. So that lamp you never use—the one shaped like a dolphin mid-twirl—won't cut the function factor, nor will it pass the next test.

Aesthetic

Choose lighting that enhances the beauty of your home...both in its level of luminance and in the light's actual appearance. Does

the soft radiance emit a sense of calm in the room? Does the physical lamp or fixture match your décor, the style of your home? (The aforementioned dolphin lamp can remain if suburban Sea World is your official theme, but otherwise...*gone*.)

Begin to look at light as a fun and essential part of your home's aesthetic appeal. An attractive home with a balance of natural and powered light has depth and texture. Properly placed lighting ensures that there is not a glare on the framed photographs that restricts the view of the image. It fills an area without stripping the room of color and ambience. And it never detracts from the style or comfort of the decor.

One day I was reading in our guest bedroom and I realized that our side table reading lamp was too high. It cast light on my book which was pleasant, but when I reached up to adjust the brightness, the high angle beamed the wattage right into my eyes...a bit like an interrogation tactic. We love conversing with our guests but don't necessarily want their true confessions. So this error in judgment was a functional problem and also an aesthetic one. This light was not at all joyful or beautiful to the eye of the book-holder who was blinded right before bedtime.

Blended

This home improvement project will bring balance and harmony to your dwelling. Blend your fragments of light so that the sources are not competing with one another and negating the effect. Consider lighting to be the visual equivalent to music as a mood-setter.

Think in terms of layering light and 1) you will notice where you need additional lighting, and 2) you will create a more interesting and natural look in your home.

If your idea of lighting is "Flip the switch and be done with it," then you will be pleasantly surprised by the impact of layering. Start small...you don't have to rewire your house to move a floor lamp so it focuses on the table where your family plays games. Next, turn on the lamp in the corner that is not as intense as the one directed at the table but not as soft as the room's ambient light. This helps balance the effect of the floor lamp. The premise of layering is not to turn on every light in the house. Rather, use lighting to suit the event, the activity, and the mood of a moment.

My sister turns off the main kitchen fixture (as soon as her husband turns it on) and uses the light sources over the sink and the stove instead. Her husband, who works for a lighting company, found this routine to be a bit annoying, if not a bit contrary. That is, until he realized she has a natural inclination toward layering. Just like that...her quirky habit was cast in good light.

And there was joy.

How to Shed Good Light

- A good rule to follow: Use a frosted bulb in frosted glass, clear bulb in clear glass.

- For outdoor lighting, frosted glass is more attractive—it camouflages the bulb best. Also, get an outdoor fixture with a bottom opening for easier bulb changes.

- Layer light. Everything from windows to a reading lamp allows you to layer the light in a room and create dimension and ambience. Here are a few definitions:

    General lighting essentially serves as daylight in a room.

    Accent lighting draws attention to the items you want to show off, such as a painting or a special room feature.

    Task lighting is for areas where focused light is required—for example, at a sink or countertop.

- If you have 8-foot ceilings, use flush fixtures. If your ceilings are higher, semi-flush or hanging fixtures are appropriate.

- In your dining room, the bottom of the light fixture should be 30 to 36 inches from table top.

- In a dining room, use a dimmer switch to avoid the glaring spotlight effect when you are eating.

- Complement your décor.

- Choose a finish that suits the style in the room, e.g., brushed nickel to match your cabinet pulls. Your paint color might change so don't base all your fixture decisions on that factor. Use the house structure and more permanent design elements as your influencers.

- Darker colors for fixture trim add richness and dimension. These are very popular right now so there are many designs, colors, and textures to choose from.

Have a Solid Foundation

FAITHFULNESS

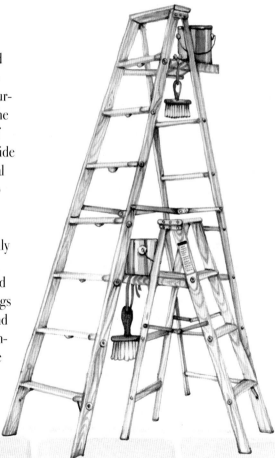

I am certain that my chiropractor would tell you to never, *never* paint the bathroom ceiling while trying to stabilize yourself with one foot on the tub ledge and the other propped up on the sink's edge. Of course, I am only guessing she would chide you mercilessly about such a hypothetical act of stupidity...if that ever happened to *you*...and *if* you happened to go see my chiropractor.

"Stand on something solid" is not only stellar advice for our safety, but also for our house's well-being. We have all heard people (or heard of people) who say things like "The house was an absolute mess and had no charm, but the structure and foundation were solid so we bought it." Since I prefer aesthetics to practicality, my immediate response is, "The house was a charmless mess? And you bought it? What *were* you thinking?" But of course, these folks understand that the foundation is a crucial element. And just as my chiropractor lectures me...er...you about having a secure foundation while painting your ceiling...any contractor would offer similar advice regarding your house.

My friend has a house with one corner of the foundation sinking. She doesn't fret at night about the house falling down, but the settling foundation means that everything in that part of the house is out of square. She can't put new snap-together flooring down because the floor isn't

But the plans of the Lord stand firm forever, the purposes of his heart through all generations.

THE BOOK OF PSALMS

level. A crack that can't be hidden has developed that runs up a wall and across the ceiling of her dining room. She can't fit the screen door on the slider because it's out of alignment. And anything that spills slides toward that corner. At first glance the foundation problem doesn't seem huge, but it affects (and limits) everything that goes on in that part of her house.

Foundations of Faith

The shifts in the foundation of our personal lives can be as initially subtle and eventually frustrating as those my friend is experiencing with

> **But as for me and my household,
> we will serve the Lord.**
>
> THE BOOK OF JOSHUA

her home. At first you notice something is "off." The things that used to line up perfectly now refuse to come together. It is during these times that we must secure our foundation on the rock of faith.

Many of us have heard reference to the Bible's take on this. It pretty much says that the man who puts faith into practice is like a man who builds a house on a rock foundation. But the one who does not apply the truths of faith is like the man who builds his house without a foundation. When the floods come...when life's trials whirl about...the house not built on solid ground will collapse.

When we choose to stand on faith, we are stabilizing our lives with a sure strength. From this place—in this stance—we can safely step up and reach out without losing our balance. We can spend time caring for our friends, tending to our marriages, building our families, and meeting the needs of others and ourselves. When we start to feel off-balance again, our faithfulness will lead us to build a life, repair the cracks, and face the faults.

Keeping our life on unshakable ground becomes a matter of maintenance. A house is no different. We must watch for signs of the shift. When we identify the beginnings of a crack in the surface of the foundation, we must faithfully tend to the repairs. Only then can we hope for our house to stand firm when the winds blow. Only then can we hope to build a future on the foundation that has been our cornerstone all along.

Foundation repairs are expensive; help avoid major problems in the future by doing a regular checkup on your home. Inspect foundation walls for cracks; these can be caused by settling, expanding tree roots, or improper drainage. Inspect and clean out your gutters regularly and be sure that the drains direct water away from the foundation.

BOB VILA
Host of the *This Old House*
Quote from www.BobVila.com

44

Home Improvement
Is Life Improvement

LOVE

When you reacquaint yourself with the spaces in your house, it is a personal homecoming. While my husband was away visiting family, I made a conscious effort to savor my entire house...not to mention my solitude.

I ate in the living room. I used my laptop in the bedroom and on the front porch. I watched DVDs in the study. I rearranged furniture late at night. I even vacuumed the unidentified room...the one that morphs between storage room, dressing room, and cat playroom. I got so lost in my personal exploration of my home that I almost missed a chance to perform the ultimate home improvement effort: sharing.

As God would have it, there were plenty of opportunities to share my home...as soon as I opened the door. A friend was going through a hard time and the guest room provided her with a place to think, and rest.

Shine

Rain

The Topiary

limon

Susie Mause

Another friend extended a gracious offer to help me work on my back yard, so we shared lots of time sweating and chatting. Yet another friend offered to come over and unload stepping stones on my birthday. (I know...I need to get out more). During this time I also hosted a few gatherings that in the past I would have avoided.

Even allowing people to help me was an act of sharing. I made the choice to invite more people into my life. Giving and receiving can be such a vulnerable exchange...but it is the work required to nurture relationships.

As I opened up my home, I was able to open up my heart during a time when I would normally just relish the chance to be alone. The advice of my wise and generous friends to "pass it on" rang true as I found one reason after another to invite others into the spaces of my home. I realized how thankful I was to have this house to offer. And gratitude is a remarkable source out of which we can offer sincere love and kindness.

Home improvement becomes life improvement when we offer others the fruits of our labor. Home improvement becomes life improvement when we see our house become a home through love.

I read within a poet's book
A word that starred the page,
"Stone walls do not a prison make,
Nor iron bars a cage."

Yes, that is true, and something more:
You'll find, where'er you roam,
That marble floors and gilded walls
Can never make a home.

But every house where Love abides
And Friendship is a guest,
Is surely home, and home, sweet, home;
For there the heart can rest.

HENRY VAN DYKE, *Home Song*

When you learn a new repair, share it with someone else. Go to a neighbor and show her how to perform garage door safety tests.... Install lever handles in your mom's home to make opening doors a little easier for her. Demonstrate to your sister how to use a fire extinguisher. Use your knowledge as a tool for improving your life as well as the lives of others.

JULIE SUSSMAN AND STEPHANIE GLAKAS-TENET
Dare to Repair